Rolling back the SWANSEA years

David Roberts

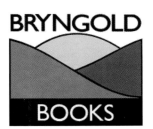

Published by Bryngold Books Ltd
100 Brynau Wood, Cimla,
Neath, South Wales SA11 3YQ.

Typesetting, layout, editing and design by Bryngold Books
Copyright © Bryngold Books 2014.

ISBN 978-1-905900-35-0

Printed and bound in Wales by Gomer Press

www.bryngoldbooks.com

About the author

David Roberts has been compiling pictorial nostalgia books for nearly two decades. His publications are widely acknowledged as a valuable contribution to the recording of the way people and places in the area once were.

A long-time journalist and latterly publisher, he worked in the Swansea Bay area for nearly 40 years, witnessing at first hand many of the events and changes his compelling books now reflect.

The culmination of his annual picture gathering is always eagerly awaited as people clamour to add to their collection, the latest in a series of books that rank as one of the best pictorial social archives in the United Kingdom.

This is David's 17th book on Swansea alongside another on the city's wartime three night's blitz and 15 others produced on its neighbouring towns of Neath and Port Talbot.

A 1984 Swansea panorama. This view would be much different today.

A big thank you

Rolling back the Swansea years is a book that has only been made possible with the help and encouragement of many people, not least all those who have shared and allowed the use of their fantastic photographs of people, places and events.

These contributions, both large and small capture times from the city's past and allow it to be seen from a different perspective, often through the eyes of those who were there, camera in hand. We are grateful for the involvement of: The South Wales Evening Post, its editor Jonathan Roberts and senior editorial assistant Pat Jones; Stephen Miles, Roy Kneath, Huw Daniel, Graham Davies, Les Saunders, Clive Williams, William Bateman, Hilary Isaac, Rita Lewis, Raymond & Dorothy Lewis, Kathryn Owens, Jodie Jones, Hilary Evans, Sandra Hayden, Alan Lloyd, Julie Cole, Steve Davies, Ashley Lovering, Geoff Rees, Delma Mainwaring, Steve Phillips, Steve & Sandra McCulloch, John Jones, Russ Thomas, Adeline Evans, Paul Smith, Colin Riddle, Gaye Mortali, Des Jeffreys, John Roberts, Anthony Owens, Peter Muxworthy, Sarah Briggs, Michael Hallett, John Griffiths, Bryndon Evans, Ken & Marie John, Bill Morris, Christine Lewis, Julie Jones, Wendie John, Vivian Davies, Silvia & Bernard Miles, Irene Willis, Roger Green, Louise Watkins, Hugh Rees, Eric Hill, Peter Nedin, Chris Taylor, Barry Jones, Roger Fordhan, Angela Gowman, Jennifer Pember and Jean Evans.

Others without whose help the book would not have appeared include Charlie Wise, Neil Melbourne and David Beynon. Finally, I must, as ever, thank my wife Cheryl for her unfailing support. Without that I am sure the task would have been far more difficult to achieve.

Share your pictures

If you have photographs of people or places in and around Swansea right up to recent times then you could play a part in recording the history of your area by sharing them in the next Swansea nostalgia book. Please telephone 01639 643961 or e-mail david.roberts@bryngoldbooks.com to discover the ways in which you can do this. Don't be shy. We would be delighted to hear from you. All photographs, transparencies, negatives, black and white or colour, of people, places, events, streets, buildings, schooldays and sport are considered whatever their age, subject or format. They are all promptly returned. We can also receive your pictures electronically. Meanwhile, if you have missed any of the previous 16 books then contact us now as some titles are still available to help complete your collection. You can also check out our other titles at
www.bryngoldbooks.com

Introduction

Rolling back the Swansea years offers a fascinating photographic slice of life in Swansea through many decades. It ensures that while its residents can look ahead in eager anticipation for what the future may hold, they can also reflect on what has gone before. As those who have known and loved the city turn its pages memories of those distant days will come flooding back.

Those who are familiar with the 16 previous books that have appeared in the consecutive years since the first edition of this reflective series will know that each one has brought a fresh crop of interesting and enlightening images. *Rolling back the Swansea years* maintains what has now become a tradition.

Just like the proud city it mirrors however, the book has gradually been evolving and its current appearance this year may be seen as a departure from previous years. Gone are the regimented chapters and date order, instead the current harvest of pictures is presented in a more relaxed fashion offering the prospect of a fresh adventure back in time on every page.

Despite this departure, the amazing pictorial moments in time shared within the cover of *Rolling back the Swansea years* are as diverse as ever. Once again there will be few who cannot claim their own personal link with at least a handful of this magnificent crop of photographs. They feature people, places, events and much more. They create an inimitable feel for the way we once were.

This is a book which will take everyone on an unbeatable excursion through the past decade and into the past century. It is a trip that is sure to be enjoyed. Sit back . . . and enjoy!

David Roberts, 2014.

The hustle and bustle that typified High Street in 1932. The pavements are thronged with people who no doubt patronised many of the independent stores that flourished along both sides of this busy shopping mecca. The trams which ferried shoppers in and out of town appear to be busy too.

A group of people admire the raised floral clock at Victoria Park, 1912.

Pupils of the Sunday School at St Paul's Church, Plasmarl, 1954.

The hot air balloon flown by the owner of and proudly proclaiming the name of popular Swansea builders merchant DAL floats across the city's docklands, late 1970s.
The industrial backdrop is provided by the BP Chemicals plant at Baglan Bay, Port Talbot.

With the Vivian Arms behind him this police officer is
directing traffic at Sketty Cross in the early 1950s.

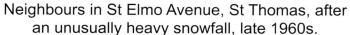

Neighbours in St Elmo Avenue, St Thomas, after
an unusually heavy snowfall, late 1960s.

The High Street department store of
Lewis Lewis acted like a magnet for
discerning shoppers for many
decades. Seen here in the early
1900s, it was just one of the big name
stores in the street.

The Tennant Canal was, in its heyday
a vital link between the coal producers
of the Neath Valley and Swansea
Docks. Much of this scene at
Port Tennant vanished under the
concrete and tarmac of the
Fabian Way dual carriageway.

11

Jack Lewis the photographer felt he was on a winner back in 1909 when he strung a banner across Castle Street proclaiming that his photographs all came with sticky backs.

The commanding statue of Sir Henry Vivian casts a watchful
eye over proceedings in Wind Street in the early 1900s.

When it came to confectionery, Athertons of Oxford Street was the place to go in 1910, judging
by the well stocked window behind this man who may even have been HC Atherton himself.

Castle Gardens, much lamented by many, seen on a sunny spring day during the mid-1960s.

Whatever your taste in cycles, there was plenty of choice
at Dan Morgan's in Oxford Street, early 1920s.

These trucks and their drivers were engaged in the removal
of spoil from Hafod tip. The vehicles owned by Evan Thomas
& Son are all Bedfords with the exception of the Commer
vehicle on the far left.

The staff of the Star grocery and provisions store, Mount Pleasant, early 1900s. Buckets and washboards appear to have been among their popular wares.

Pupils of Dunvant Infants School during their Nativity Play, 2001.

Pupils and teachers of form 5A Swansea Girls' High School, at Townhill playing fields with hockey sticks, January 30, 1951.

Staff of Singleton Hospital's CSSD department before setting off on a
charity walk to raise money for cot death syndrome research, 1980s.

Heavy snow meant a break in their regular routine for staff at Swansea Garden Centre, Blackpill.
The huge snowman was the result of their efforts. The garden centre closed in the mid-1980s.

Looking towards the city centre along Fabian Street at its junction with Lewis Street, St Thomas, early 1960s.

An articulated lorry carrying a load of steel girders struggles and fails to negotiate the corner of Cambrian Place and Gloucester Place, 1968.

Adelaide Street, early 1960s, before construction of the building that for many decades housed the South Wales Evening Post offices.

Onlookers surround the ketch Lenora of Barnstaple which ran aground at Langland on November 19, 1913.

The Cape Horner public house, St Thomas, December 1963 and **RIGHT:** The familiar tiled sign that for decades greeted passers-by.

Not so plain sailing

A tug alongside the ill-fated trawler Barry Castle which sank at its moorings on August 23, 1949 while loading 60 tons of ice at the South Dock Basin. She was refloated the next day.

The Kingsway roundabout played a major part in Swansea's traffic management for many decades. Initially it was a magnificent floral spectacle when this scene was captured in the summer of 1960. Princess Way can be seen to the right and College Street straight ahead.
INSET: A view down the Kingsway, showing the C&A fashion chain store at the junction of the Kingsway and Park Street, May, 1952.

Wind Street, 1909, showing the impressive curved glass roofed portico of the Metropole Hotel. **TOP RIGHT:** a view further up the street showing part of the legendary Ben Evans department store. **RIGHT:** The Post Office, one of the focal points of the street as it appeared in 1903.

Wind of change

The helter skelter that towered above Swansea Beach at The Slip for many years and proved a popular attraction for generations of children, early 1900s.

Two different guises and two different poses of the giant-sized cartoon-like characters that for many years were a familiar sight at the entrance to Mumbles Pier.

On a winter's afternoon in the late 1950s this Stanier 8F locomotive is waiting to proceed near Wind Street Junction on the former Vale of Neath Railway high level lines that linked Swansea Victoria station with Swansea's main docks complex.

A group of retired BT Swansea employees enjoy a holiday trip, 2003.

Student nurses at Swansea General Hospital, 1961.

Crowds enjoy the sunshine at the Royal National Eisteddfod of Wales, Singleton Park, 1982.

Just one of the parties that filled many Swansea streets in July 1977 to mark the Silver Jubilee of Queen Elizabeth II. This glorious table of goodies was laid out in Alexandra Terrace, Brynmill.

Party time

This is how some of the residents of St Elmo Avenue, St Thomas commemorated the Silver Jubilee of Queen Elizabeth II in July 1977.

Vehicles prepare to turn off Oystermouth Road into West Way, on June 29, 1983. The gasworks site in the background is now Tesco's Marina store.

Passengers queuing at Singleton Street bus station, early 1980s.

The first Park and Ride site at Landore. In the background and still under construction, the now vanished Morfa Athletics stadium on December 18, 1982.

A South Wales Transport double decker is forced to take a detour on Route 74 on June 6, 1963 with police officers diverting traffic on Gower Road.

Oxford Street looking towards Princess Way, mid-1960s.

One of the
pretty carnival
queens and
her attendants
at Bishopston
Carnival,1990.

School pupils at
Three Crosses,
1920s.

A two car Mumbles Train heads along Oystermouth Road in the early 1950s.

A very young skiffle group at the rear of Port Tennant Road, 1958. The Fabian Way dual carriageway runs through this spot now.

This is how they delivered the milk from Gambold's Graig Dairy at North Hill to the doors of local customers in the early 1900s.

A view of Wind Street across Victoria Road and the Little Wind Street car park from the front of Swansea Museum on April 28, 2002.

A passer-by watches two young lads, deep in concentration, during a game of marbles in the street at Llwyn Derw, Fforestfach, during the 1930s.

The Palmer and Evans garage and petrol filling station, Philips Parade, early 1950s.

Families at Vivian Street, Hafod, gather for a victory tea to celebrate VJ Day on August 15, 1945.

The gasworks, Oystermouth Road. Much of this site is now occupied by a Tesco supermarket. Garden Street multi-storey car park occupies the bottom right hand corner of the view and Gregor Bros. timber yard and the South Dock are visible at the top.

43

Swansea's parks and entertainment committee members prepare for their annual tour of the city, 1968.

The pedestrian subway which linked Wind Street and Somerset Place, 2010.

Two Sandfields streets which fell victim to flash flooding in 1972.

Adelaide Street in the early 1960s. The empty, walled space on the right, was all that remained of the Adelaide Hotel which was destroyed by bombing in the Second World War. The site later became home to the offices of the South Wales Evening Post newspaper.

The Big Apple at Mumbles in the 1990s. For generations the seaside hotspot has been a popular landmark with locals and visitors alike.

Photographer and historian Roy Kneath with the carving referred to as the Swansea Devil. It originally adorned a building opposite St Mary's Church before vanishing for many years. Roy was involved in tracking it down to a Gloucester garage and returning it to the city. It was discreetly placed in the Quadrant shopping centre where it can still be seen.

The footbridge of Swansea Bay station was the vantage point for this townward glimpse of the Slip bridge and the swimming baths alongside, in the early 1960s.

The North Dock Basin, former berthing place for many of the ships which transported grain from around the world to the Weaver's Mill grain store that stands alongside, late 1940s.

Usherettes and sales staff at the Albert Hall on its last night as a cinema, 1977.

Scaffolding lines one side of Lower Union Street as construction of Swansea Market nears completion, 1959. Opposite is the Peter Jones cafeteria, a favourite lunchtime rendezvous for shoppers for decades.

Children enjoying the delights of fishing in the lake at Singleton Park during the late 1950s.

The semi-derelict, but still imposing
Palace Theatre building, 2003.

The crew of the paddle steamer Brighton which operated from Pockett`s Wharf, on the River Tawe, on September 26, 1901.The Brighton was built in 1878 and acquired by Pockett's in 1896 operating Bristol Channel sailings for 19 years until being requisitioned for First World War service in 1915. After this she was sold to Turkish owners, being broken up there in 1927. Pockett's Wharf owes its name to James Wathan Pockett who relocated his business, Pockett's Bristol Channel Steam Packet Company, from the North Dock to the South Dock basin in 1871.

Bishop Gore School's cricket X1, 1954 with teachers and headmaster.

A magnificent array of 1950s and 1960s vehicles fills the temporary that existed between the car sales premises of Glanfield Lawrence and St Mary's Church in 1971. The scene was captured from scaffolding on the nearly complete Quadrant shopping centre. Fashion chain C&A later occupied this site and it is still a fashion store, but under the New Look banner. A close look at the rooftops shows vehicles stored or parked by the motor dealer.

Not quite 'legs 11' but these young women seem to have been enjoying themselves at Swansea University's Rag Ball in 1959.

The lavish interior of the Glynn Vivian art gallery, Alexandra Road, prior to its refurbishment.

A rare chance to sample the view out of Cockett railway tunnel, mid-1980s.

Staff of the Castle Cinema, their friends and family all set for a day out.

Pupils at Dumbarton House School, 1971.

Copies of the latest edition of the Adelaide Street-based South Wales Evening Post are hurried into a familiar fleet of maroon-painted Morris 1000 vans to be dispersed across the city, 1968.

A group of Swansea bus enthusiasts alongside a line up of South Wales Transport
AEC Regent V buses on their last day of service with the company, 1983.

The Sunday School scripture class of
Aenon Baptist Church, Morriston, 1954.

Bridging the gap

The central support for the sail bridge across the River Tawe is deftly lowered into place by a giant crane on March 30, 2003. The background shows a hive of activity of construction linked to the city's SA1 development.

Construction work underway on the towering DVLA building at Clase, Morriston, August 3, 1972.

Swansea Castle dominates the right of this view up Castle Lane, 1860.

The concourse at High Street railway station, late 1920s.

South Wales Transport Bus company conductress, Lucy Athernought who together with fellow conductress Lil Stainton celebrated 25 years service with the company, in 1977, pictured with company officials and fellow members of staff.

At High Street station, locomotive 4981 Abberley Hall backs down onto coaches
which will form the 1.50pm departure to Carmarthen, late 1950s.

The floral clock that for decades was an eye-catching feature at Victoria Park.

A civic greeting for swimmers who took part in a
Boxing Day dip in the sea at Bracelet Bay, Mumbles.

If any photograph could serve as an epitaph to the Mumbles Railway then this view, from the pier in the late summer of 1959 must surely be it.

Looking across Langland Bay with its rows of Beach Huts, mid-1950s.

Swansea's temporary market in 1954. The outdoor gathering of stalls which sprung up after the wartime bombing of the building served shoppers through rain and shine until 1960 when the current market was opened.

A fascinating view of Mumbles Road, Blackpill from the railway bridge that crossed over the road at this point, early 1960s. Heading into the town centre are two South Wales Transport AEC Regent V buses while parked at the roadside is an Evening Post delivery van.

A petrol filling station in the Strand and behind, Welcombe House office block, mid-1960s.

Construction work underway on the former David Evans department store, early 1950s.
In front work has yet to begin on the delightful green oasis that was Castle Gardens.

Vehicles at the busy Fforestfach Cross traffic intersection, mid-1970s.

With the spoils of their day's sport are participants in the
Jones-Bennett Shoot at Kittle Gower, February 22, 1912.

Shoppers in Oxford Street, Swansea, July 1973.

Old greenhouses at Clyne Gardens, one of Swansea's botanical jewels, 2008.

All smiles for the photographer from this group of Swansea Girl Guides who were enjoying a trip to the beach at Blackpill.

There was no traffic, but plenty of people to be found in College Street in 1969 when it was paved and filled with giant flower beds and seating. These two views in spring and summer of that year are looking towards the Dragon Hotel.

The Bush Hotel, 233 High Street, early 1900s.

Don't rain on my parade! Well it definitely did rain on the day of Morriston carnival in 1976. No one however was prepared to let it dampen their spirits. Star guests, locals who lined the route and almost everyone else involved appears to have been determined to have a great time. Main attraction of the day was popular actor and comedian Clive Dunn, best known for his role as Lance-Corporal Jack Jones in the popular BBC sitcom Dad's Army.

A brolly good day out!

A quiet day at St David's Precinct, April 6, 2003.

Youngsters from Derwen Fawr enjoy the delights of a birthday party, 1981.

This group of Cubs and Scouts certainly seem a happy band,
particularly the three who have just received awards!

Somerset Place with the imposing architecture of
Swansea's former Guildhall on the right, 1968.

Most of the former gasworks site has been cleared and preliminary work is underway on the construction of Tesco's Marina store.

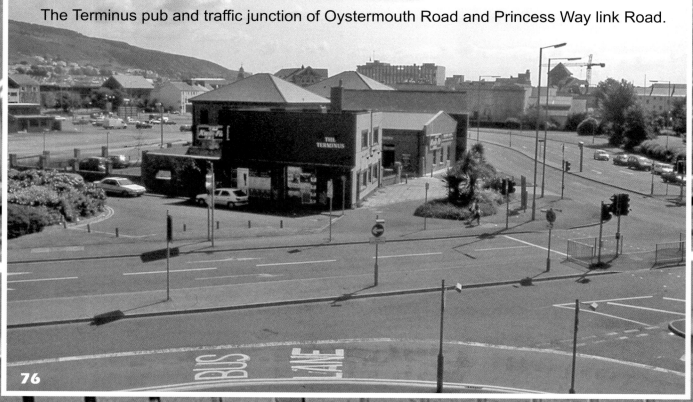

The Terminus pub and traffic junction of Oystermouth Road and Princess Way link Road.

Some of the high level railway arches at the South Dock.

The former lightship Helwick with a maritime backdrop far different to that which exists at Swansea's South Dock marina today, 1976.

A group of children at Parkmill, Gower, early 1950s.

A class of pupils at Olchfa School, 1991.

Pupils of Terrace Road School enjoying a lesson during the 1970s.

Two of the South Dock marina's popular landmarks: the Pumphouse restaurant and the Helwick lightship, 1983.

Putting some bite into Bishopston Carnival, 1976.

Coronation cowboy capers

Not a horse in sight, but these young Swansea cowboys still seem to have been enjoying themselves back in 1953 dressed in Wild West outfits during celebrations of the Coronation of Queen Elizabeth II.

Musical magnet

Making music and enjoying through day and night at the Heineken Festival, Singleton Park, August 7, 1993. Headlining events were the Manic Street Preachers.

Shoppers crossing busy Princess Way, 1970s.

Townhill Residents Association with young performers
at a Nativity play staged for them, December 1973.

A fine vista of Oxford Street, across Castle Gardens, 1972.

A mixed freight train heads past Swansea Bay Station, St Helen's, with Mumbles Road on the right, 1964.

City in the snow

Wind street in 1982 . . .

86

Snow across the city. An atmospheric dusting for Townhill in 2005 . . .

. . . and Mount Pleasant in 2010.

One of the many successful Ostreme fetes at Mumbles.

Youngsters enjoying one of the attractions at Cadle School fete 1976.

Local Brownies attend a civic book launch at
Swansea Museum, October 2, 2010.

Under starter's orders.

Manselton
pancake
race 1976

Tossing it
with style.

Almost
losing it.

Heading for an exciting finish!

Ernest Griffiths in his shop at Sketty Cross, 1965.

A group of workmen at a city council depot, mid-1970s.

The Celtic Pride ferry prepares to leave King's Dock, on March 3, 1991.

The Swansea to Cork ferryship Innisfallen arrives at the ferryport on her maiden voyage on the route, May 2, 1969.

The MV Superferry at Swansea Ferryport on March 7, 1993.

Celtic links across the sea

On a sunny evening in July 1990, the Irish Sea ferry Ionian Sun arrives at the mouth of the River Tawe.

At King's Dock, after its inaugural sailing from Cork on April 16, 1987 is the ferry Celtic Pride.

Royal Mail staff loading the final Travelling Post Office train to leave High Street station, on Friday July 25, 2003.

Some of the sorting bays aboard the train.

It's a different station, but the same story as the last 6.30pm York Mail train heads out of Swansea Victoria station on June 13, 1964. The end of another era.

A civic salute for successful sand sculptors on Swansea beach.

Racing ahead with an eye-catching design.

The Lord Mayor joins crowds of onlookers to welcome Father Christmas to the city in 1973. ABOVE: A festive David Evans store and shoppers on the hunt for gifts.

The frozen fountain at Castle Gardens, late 1950s.

Scouts, Cubs, Brownies and Guides all did their bit to make sure that Swansea districts Gang Show was a huge success in 1973.

The ill-fated dry ski slope at Morfa, 2000.

The Parade at Southend, 1898.

Looking towards the city centre from the Slip bridge, 1982.

Mumbles Pier during a period of renovation work, 1980s. Even in this state it was still a popular attraction . . . with seagulls, at least!

Looking up . . .

A view of the city from the docks before the demolition of Weaver's mill and nearby buildings.

Swansea Docks and construction work on the SA1 development looking down from Townhill.

down . . .

and through

The South Dock marina framed by
the arch at its westernmost end.

Maritime mirrors

The Meridian Tower, mirrored by the retreating tide on Swansea Beach, 2010.

Apartment buildings in the SA1 development
reflected in dockland waters, 2008.

A mirror image of more SA1 waterside homes, 2008.

The offices of Unifloc, Adelaide Street, early 1960s. The offices of the South Wales Evening Post newspaper had yet to be built, opposite.

The whitewashed Norwegian Church forms the centrepiece of this panorama looking towards the Prince of Wales Dock, taken after a dusting of snow in the late 1990s. As part of the redevelopment of the SA1 site, in 2004 the church was carefully dismantled, piece by piece, and moved to its present location alongside the dock, where it was re-erected and restored. It is now a jeweller's studio and gallery.

Hidden away from most eyes, these are the backs of properties in lower Wind Street. In the distance can be seen Swansea Museum and the Evening Post offices, 2002.

An atmospheric view of the gantry that supported floodlights at Vetch Field, November 9, 2010 shortly before they were dismantled.

Looking from St Thomas, across the River Tawe swing bridge towards part of the sprawling Weaver's flour mill complex on the opposite bank of the river. The Midland Railway station is above and to the right of this picture taken in the early 1950s.

Manselton School Choir, 1951.

Tailors at work in Hodges Menswear factory, Fforestfach, 1953.

Never mind the weather, as long as we're together! Brownies and Guides brave the wet weather to welcome Chief Guide Lady Baden Powell to Swansea. Umbrellas were definitely a vital part of the kit that day.

A visit from Santa in summer? Well, it happened at Eastside carnival in 1993. And just to make sure everyone saw him he brought along a double too!

Making a splash

Crowds watch the antics of some of the successful, and not so successful competitors in one of the exciting Mumbles raft races.

Employees of the Imperial Aluminium Industries works,
Waunarlwydd, gather for a presentation, possibly to a
newly qualified apprentice, late 1950s.

Young cyclists prepare to tackle the challenges
of the BMX track at the west side of the
original Leisure Centre, 2002.

Buildings at Castle Street undergo restoration
following wartime bomb damage, 1950.

A youngster enjoys a moment of fun in the rusting remains of this once majestic car found in the undergrowth at Olchfa House, Sketty, shortly before its demolition, mid-1990s.

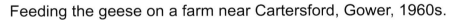

Feeding the geese on a farm near Cartersford, Gower, 1960s.

Mirroring the Teddy Boy fashions of the 1950s these lads were snapped with two appropriately dressed girl friends outside The Park pub, Portland Street, 1978.

A group of the young Queens who brought a regal touch to Loughor fete, 1973.

The steam ship Tours, high and dry at Deepslade Bay, Gower. The vessel ran aground in November 1918 when bound for Swansea to load coal for Nantes, France. She ran aground broadside and was successfully refloated on June 29, 1919.

Part of the delivery vehicle fleet of shipping purveyors C Clode & Sons together with drivers, proudly lined up outside Swansea Guildhall, mid-1950s. Either side of the vans and lorries are two of the company's cars.

Members of the Swansea District Collieries Rescue Association, complete with their response vehicle, early 1920s.

An atmospheric scene at Swansea Victoria Station, early 1960s.

Construction work underway on West Glamorgan County Hall, Oystermouth Road, 1982. The building is now Swansea Civic Centre.

One of the cooks with equipment installed in a new kitchen at Swansea Docks, early 1960s.

A welcoming party greets the arrival of Her Majesty the Queen Mother at High Street station, May 28, 1959. She was attending the official opening of the rebuilt, war-damaged St Mary's Church.

Prince Edward takes time to speak to a group of pupils during a visit to Olchfa School, 1992.

The Royal yacht, HMS Victoria and Albert at Swansea Docks,1920.

Inside the council chamber at Swansea Guildhall during the ceremony at which Councillor Alan Lloyd became Lord Mayor, March 2009.

There are times when even our first citizen deserves some relaxation! Lord Mayor Howard Morgan concentrates deeply during a game of bingo at one of his engagements, during his busy civic year.

Looking across Swansea Bay towards the city centre from Mumbles, 1982.

Looking down on a section of Carmarthen Road, August 22, 2002.

Centenary celebration presentations to staff in the canteen of Lewis Lewis' High Street store.

A young photographer gets some tips from his dad at Brynmill Park, 1962.

127

Hugh Cheley, a security guard at the Morganite company's Morriston plant with his guard dog, alongside a location plan of the site, 1989.

Motor neurone society supporters at a fundraising party pictured with boxers Neville Mead, Barry McGuigan and Welsh comedian Stan Stennett, early 1990s.

The former Addis factory at Morfa, with the
Shertzer Lift Bridge in the foreground, 2002.

Immersing themselves in the world of Olde Tyme Music Hall
was a source of enjoyment for these Swansea folk.

An outdoor game of bingo was one of the attractions at the summer fete organised at the Ford Motor Company's Jersey Marine plant in 1976.

Remember the bear at the No. 10 public house in upper Union Street? Well it seems he got a little thirsty in the 1970s!

Night-time excitement on the illuminated Giant Wheel at Swansea's Winter Wonderland attraction, 2007.

Pupils of class 2 at Lonlas Welsh School, late 1950s.

Schoolday snapshots

Pupils of Cwmrhydyceirw Primary School, July 10, 2006.

These children were lucky enough to meet up with a group of popular Disney characters at the Quadrant Shopping Centre, 1981.

Participants on one of the floats in a Swansea Scouts' carnival.

Shoppers in Oxford Street, late 1950s. **Inset:** High Street gets ready for Christmas in the mid-1970s.

Her Majesty the Queen Mother attending the re-dedication ceremony of St Mary's Church, May, 1959. **BELOW:** the church choir which took part in the ceremony.

Looking across Victoria Road towards the remains of arches that once carried the high level rail line from Swansea's main docks to the South Dock, with Hancock's brewery behind, early 1970s.
INSET: a South Wales Transport bus passes the building as it heads for its terminus at the Exchange, early 1950s.

Looking up The Strand towards High Street railway station, 1937.

Doctors, nurses and patients alike all received a surprise tonic when film star couple Richard Burton and Elizabeth Taylor turned up to visit a relative receiving treatment at Singleton Hospital on November 21, 1975.

Fancy dress fun for these youngsters at a party during the early 1960s.

A group of Ravenhill-based South Wales Transport employees during a retirement function held after the company's absorption of United Welsh bus services, early 1970s.

Plenty of people, but no traffic. This unusual vista of High Street was captured in May, 1959 on the day that Her Majesty the Queen Mother visited Swansea for the re-dedication of St Mary's Church after it had been rebuilt following wartime bomb damage. **RIGHT:** A little more traffic in High Street, 1958.

On the campaign trail, Screaming Lord Sutch blowing his own election trumpet in Mumbles livening up the local battle for votes.

There appears to have been much activity in the grounds of Penllergare House on the day this picture was taken in the early 1900s.

Swansea bay promenade during the construction of the Meridian Tower, 2007.

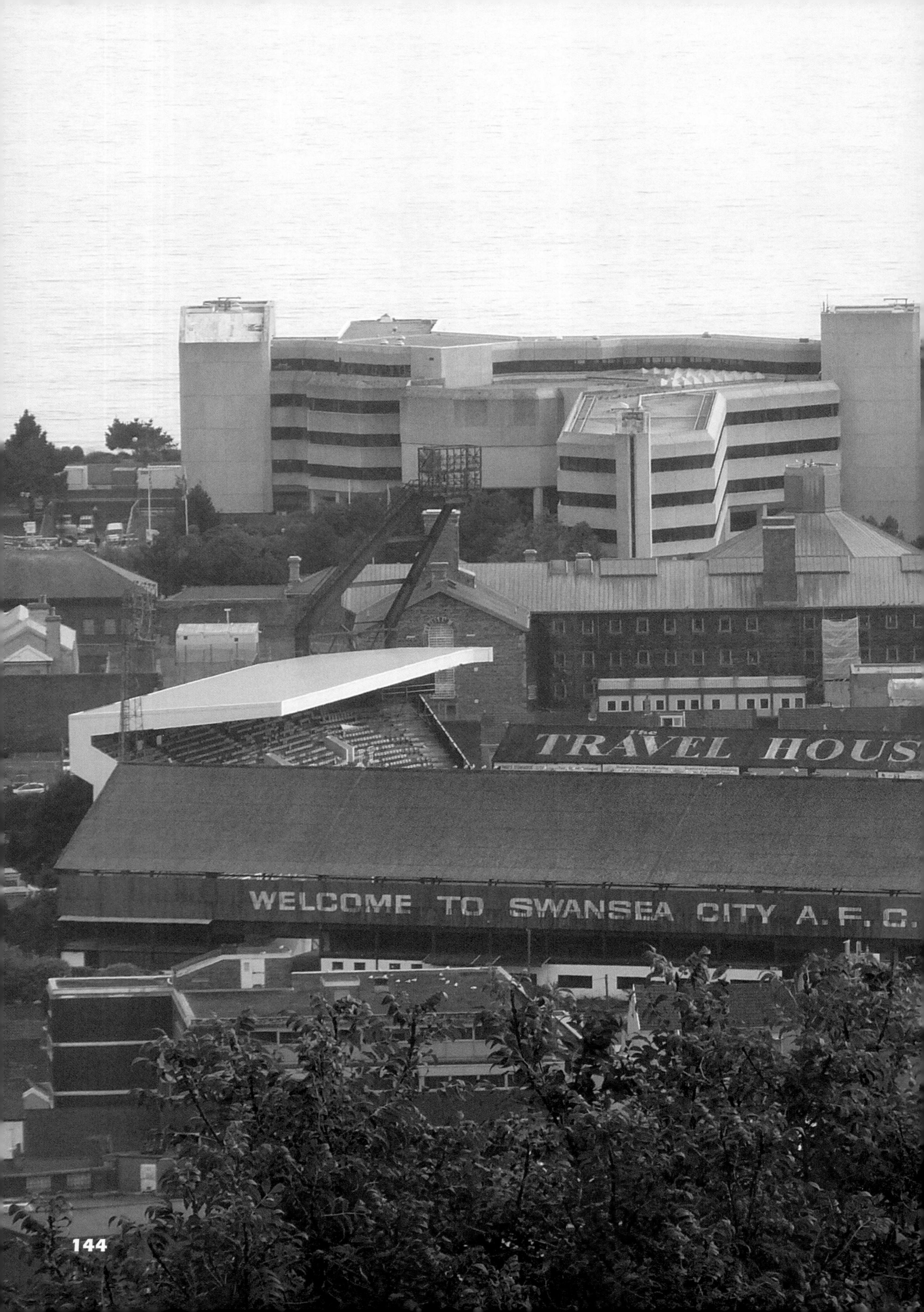
TRAVEL
WELCOME TO SWANSEA CITY A.F.C.

Looking over the Vetch Field, former home of Swansea City Football Club, Swansea Prison and the Civic Centre, 2007.

Mobbed by hordes of screaming teenagers, members of
the Bay City Rollers pop group leave the Dragon Hotel
after playing to a packed audience in the city, 1975.

Fans of pop group Take That
all set for their visit to
Swansea on July 20,1993.

A Hunslett 0-6-0 tank locomotive No. 4 of 1899 origin at Oystermouth in the mid-1920s hauls a Mumbles Train. There is an interesting line of coal wagons in the background.

Reconstruction work underway at High Street station, June 15, 1926.

Stairways to Heaven? The link between Neath Road and Dinas Street, Plasmarl, 1987 and right, Dickslade, Mumbles, 1975.

Wind blown sand almost covers the site of the former Swansea Bay railway station, January 30, 1968.

Neath Road, Landore, summer, 1976.

Exchange buildings, Adelaide Street, late 1990s.

British Road Services lorry drivers at their North Dock depot, 1950s.

The boating lake at Singleton Park, mid-1970s.

Amazingly in 1958 this lorry-mounted publicity dragon, on a tour of Wales, following a stint at the Empire Games and Ebbw Vale Eisteddfod is seen on the very spot where the Dragon Hotel would be built two years later.

Members of St Thomas Church Youth Club on a visit to St Athan youth village, early 1970s.

The Dragon Hotel overlooks
the green oasis that was
Kingsway roundabout, 1962.

The floral clock at Victoria Gardens
promotes the Festival of Britain, 1951.

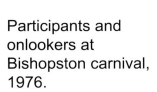

Participants and
onlookers at
Bishopston carnival,
1976.

Kenneth Peter Hardman's marriage to Maureen Francis Cole
at St Joseph's Church, Greenhill, January 1949.

Sketty Park Estate, still under construction, spring 1962.

A graveyard for unwanted vehicles at Burrows Place, near the current Dylan Thomas Centre, late 1980s. This site is now occupied by a surface car park alongside the River Tawe.

Roadworks underway at Gendros, 1969.

This group of Uplands youngsters is making music to celebrate the Silver Jubilee of Queen Elizabeth II, July 1977.

Morfa Athletics Stadium, viewed from the opposite bank of the River Tawe, where the Liberty Stadium now stands, January 2, 2002,

A GPO cable laying gang at their Strand depot, 1957.

One of the upturned, upper sections of a scrapped Mumbles Railway car lies unceremoniously on the trackside opposite Christ Church, Oystermouth Road, 1960. The diesel locomotive behind is hauling the lower deck of the car.

Newton Road, Mumbles, October 1981.

A special party was held at the Social Services Centre, Sketty during the mid-1970s to say farewell to one of its members, Miss Joyce, who was emigrating to Canada at the age of 80. Among those with Miss Joyce were Lord Mayor and Lady Mayoress of Swansea, Councillor and Mrs Mike Murphy; Social Services staff and regular members of the centre.

Cefn Hengoed School's first year soccer team, winners of the Welsh Biscuits Cup in 1980 with an aggregate score of 5 - 1. A total of 255 schools took part in the event.

The Kingsway, with a policeman on traffic point duty at its junction with Union Street, mid-1950s.

The popular group Seatown Morning on the cab of one of the Mumbles Railway cars, about which they made their first record, February, 1973.

A group of women at Cefn Road, Bonymaen, before setting off for a day out, early 1950s.

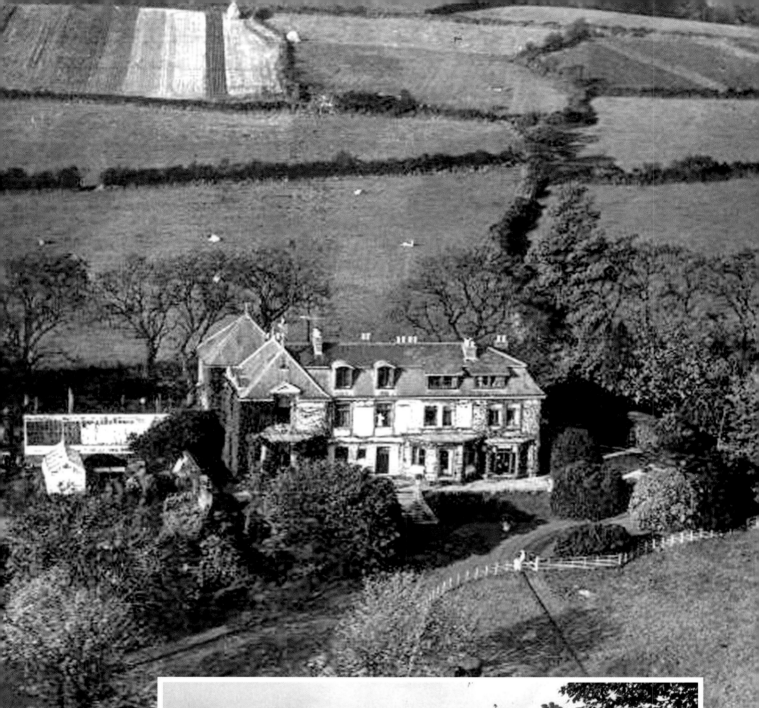

The National childrens' Home, Killay and above, a panorama of the grounds it stood in as a former mansion house. Much of this land has now been overtaken by modern housing development.

Some of the 45 members of Swansea's Morris family who set off together by coach for Cardiff and the Capitol Cinema to see the film The Sound of Music, 1965. Unsurprisingly the coach was operated by Morris Bros, the well-known transport operators with links to the family.

Students and tutors of West Glamorgan Theatre School at Danycoed Education Centre, Blackpill, during a rehearsal session for one of their mid-1980s productions.

A young lad proudly polishes his dad's car outside his home, early 1950s.

163

A view of the interior of Kilvey Church, July 1975.

Members of Sketty Church Choir, together with other members of the congregation, 1924.

The entrance to a former Swansea Market at Orange Street, and alongside, Orange Street Brewery, 1870.

Looking across Rotherslade Bay towards Langland Bay, 1920s.

A sailing vessel in the South Dock, 1910 and **INSET:** a close-up of the pump house and bridge that existed before installation of the swing bridge.

The Strand, looking towards Swansea Castle, 1860.

High Street and the Cameron Arms.
This was the terminus for trams that ran
from here to Cwmbwrla and Ynysforgan.

Christmas shopping in Oxford Street, 1982.

Some of the crowd that attended the fete organised by St Paul's Church Sketty, 1976.

Heavy snow in 1982 brought disruption and inconvenience across the country. Here, a queue forms behind a van delivering fresh fruit and vegetables to Swansea Market. **BELOW:** an even longer queue forms outside Christie's Hot Bread Kitchen across the road in Lower Union Street.

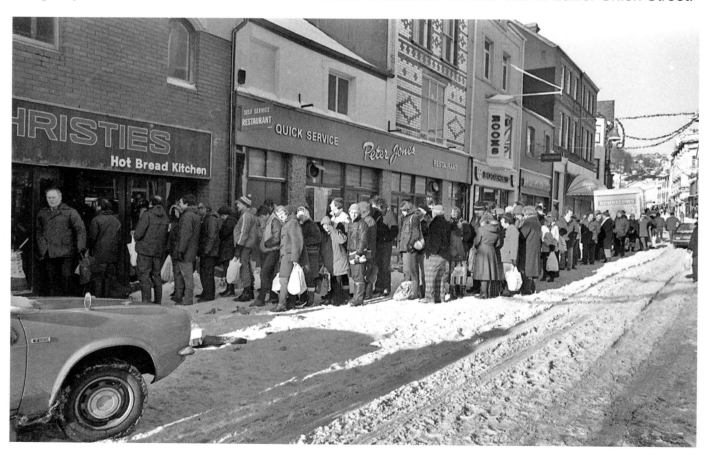

Participants in the Mumbles fun run, 1982.

A 1940s wartime Swansea wedding with the groom proudly wearing his naval uniform.

An idyllic view of the Mumbles train at Southend taken from the footbridge over the line, 1959.

Pupils of class J1A, Cwm Junior mixed school,
Bonymaen, with their teacher and headteacher, 1960.

The shopping centre at Gower Road, Killay before
construction of the precinct, early 1950s.

A new English Electric Type 3 locomotive passes over the High Level railway bridge at the lower end of Wind Street, while below, an unpainted 'silver' South Wales Transport double decker bus emerges from under the same bridge, heading for its terminus at the Exchange, 1963.

Port Tennant Road, Port Tennant, late 1973.

The sign warns 'Do not queue on the road', but with Christmas approaching in December 1990 these motorists seem intent on hanging on to their bid for a parking space in the Garden Street multi-storey car park despite the warning.

Loading anthracite at No. 4 Quay, King's Dock, on January 11, 1986, is the Hamburg-registered MV Baltic Winter.

Two ages of coal exporting infrastructure at King's Dock, on February 17, 1987. In the foreground is No. 12 Hoist, destined to be used for the last time just a few days later, while in the background, the MV Brynmore loads containers, some with coal, before her first sailing from Swansea to Belfast on that afternoon's tide. The hoist was one of 15 built in the Prince of Wales and Kings Docks by Vickers Armstrong and commissioned by the Great Western Railway in 1933. The last two in use finally reached the end of their days in 1987.

For many years the only two commodities handled at the Prince of Wales Dock, were fish and sand. Seen here is the fishing vessel Jill and in the background Hoveringham II, a sand dredger, February 8, 1988.

This is the road that linked Swansea with Jersey Marine and Neath before the construction of the Fabian Way dual carriageway and the bridge that carried this busy traffic artery over the railway into Kings Dock. This view, in 1951, is looking towards Briton Ferry. The traffic is being held up to allow the passage of a freight train, a regular occurrence in days when the docks were a hive of activity.

Nurses and the recovering wounded servicemen in their charge on the roof of Swansea's YMCA building, 1918.

Lester, the faithful horse of milkman Mr Davies, of Cadle Mill Farm, takes a break from his labours in the early 1950s. Apparently he was quite fond of Bourbon biscuits!

An aerial view of
Swansea's busy
city centre,
mid-1970s.
Many of its
landmarks are
clearly visible.

The back lane of Wern Terrace, Port Tennant, 1973.

Diesel locomotive 47815, named Abertawe Landore to commemorate the 150th anniversary of the opening of the South Wales Railway to Swansea in June 1850 together with some of the Landore depot staff who were responsible for its repainting, June 30, 2000.

There was no shortage of passengers for this bus to Clase when it called at the stop in Belle Vue Way, early 1960s.

Viewed across what would become Castle Gardens, this is Boots the Chemist's store under construction on Princess Way, May 1952. It was the first major store to be built as part of Swansea's post-war rebuilding.

Steaming ahead

Above: A Stanier 'Black 5' locomotive leaves Paxton Street engine sheds, March 18, 1958.

Left: A Standard Class 5 locomotive 73025 awaits departure from Swansea Bay station on the last leg of its journey to Swansea Victoria from Shrewsbury, April 4, 1963.

Below: Tiverton Castle is assisted by a pannier tank locomotive on the loop to west Wales at Landore with the 'down' North Mail, February 20, 1957.

Below Left: A Swansea Victoria to Pontarddulais train at Mumbles Road station, near Blackpill, late afternoon, May 14, 1964.

Looking towards Port Tennant Road, Port Tennant and beyond the skyward pointing cranes of Swansea Docks, from the foot of Kilvey Hill. The former Marcroft wagon repair works is on the left.

An interesting eastwards panorama looking towards St Thomas, December 2007. Among changes most noticeable here today would be the lack of greenery separating inbound and outbound traffic. Along with the trees and shrubs fronting the nearby Sainsbury's store it was removed in 2013 to allow construction of the Boulevard scheme. Ironically this was aimed at creating what was described as a vibrant, tree-lined street between the River Tawe bridges and Princess Way.

Looking down the back lane that separates Pant Street
and Ysgol Street, Port Tennant, 1973.

A Special visitor at the Children's Ward at
Swansea General Hospital, Phillips Parade, 1950.

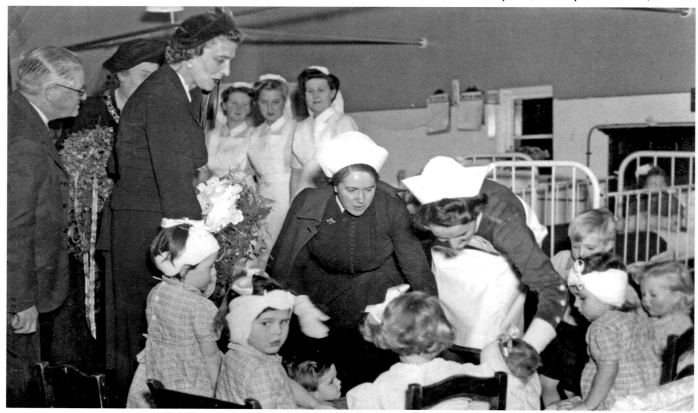

Players and officials of Swansea Town Football Club
with the spoils of a successful 1913-14 season.

Surface parking occupies the site of what became the C&A
fashion store and Quadrant Shopping Centre, early 1970s.

Looking into Morris Lane, St Thomas from Thomas Street, 1973. The building on the left was the one-time Pictorium, later Scala cinema which opened in 1913 and closed in 1934. The building later became a Dunlop Tyres depot and was demolished in 1978.

Some of the staff of RM Douglas Construction who were involved in the building of Velindre Tinplate Works, 1954.

A moment of hope for Swansea Town players in their
FA Cup Fourth Round match against Arsenal at
Highbury, London, on January 28, 1950. Arsenal were
2 - 1 winners and went on to meet Liverpool in the final.
Cost of the game's programme . . . just 6d!

Pupils of class I3A, Pennard County Primary School with their teacher, 1978.

PENNARD
COUNTY PRIMARY SCHOOL

An atmospheric damp autumn evening view of Mumbles Road at The Slip bridge, mid-1950s.